Freedom Rings

Author Desiree Lane

I admire Patrick Henry, 'Give me Liberty or give me death'. It is phrases such as these that instill within us the value of an American system of democracy. However, the cost of such freedom as it may be equated with death may come at such a price, as freedom may be a prerequisite of death. My father, grandfather, uncles and cousins were military servicemen. I traveled the world with my family and explored 80% of the United States before the age of majority. This book is my inspirations, betrayals, aspirations, and achievements. Had it cost me my life it may have been penned by a biographer, but as I am yet quick I will be its author and finisher.

I was a child of five curious to discover the world. It became a source of entertainment to the masses of parishioners to attend the Sunday morning worship service. The pastor's word was aptly punctuated with a "weeellll" or an "aaaammmeeeeen" by his young daughter. But, when the choir sang the young and old were both swayed by the emotional shouting coming from this amicable youth. Needless to say when ushers came around it was both to collect an offering as well as resuscitate many who had fainted. The scriptures were more than inspiration to me but they were a way of life. From an early age I was enchanted by my father's animated services. Throngs of people of all ages, genders, and ethnicities gathered to hear him speak.

When the time came for the shipmen to leave I was not prepared to see my father go. He was a deacon and Rear Admiral and well respected in the community. News cameras were there and many well wishers but it was the young girl that captivated his attention and held it until it was time to depart. He would hold me high in the air and point out the uttermost parts of the ship and explain in detail what was taking place aboard the enormous vessel. Although, much of this was difficult to comprehend I stood in awe as the monstrosity chimed and buzzed. My amazement was quickly replaced by anxiety however, at the realization in that it would be almost a year before I saw the enigmatic preacher again. Pa, that is what I called him Papa he was a stocky, grey haired heavily bearded southern boy turned elite military Green Beret. He served with some of the greatest politicians of our time. During this period we were stationed in a bustling southern town close to the shipyards that allowed passage of the armed military vessels. Reagan and the war on drugs were beginning to take shape.

There was not an inkling of a clue as to the tumultuous scandals that were to unfold over the next decade. The dismantling of the USSR, Iran-Contra affair, and ultimately my parents divorce. But, before any of these things were to take place we would all look forward to the upcoming fall because the Marine Corp ball was eminent.

The Marine Corp ball was an illustrious red carpet affair that brought out celebrity of every caliber. It was the upper echelons annual political soirée' that was *the* induction to the avant' garde as it were. During, this time my family which is African American held an influential role in politics and Papa was considering his own political aspirations post military. There were few African American families in our golfing country club community and this was not a fact that was overlooked. Each year the few families made tentative arrangements to gather together for a Kwanzaa celebration. We eagerly anticipated the holiday seasons primarily because much of the year was spent on literary competitions, gymnastics lessons, swimming lessons, and the like. There was not a spare moment to reflect upon what was taking place. The expectations of community leaders were to be spotless and excellence was evident. There were the lawyers, doctors, military; Jews, Catholics, nannies, and all of these people were a part of our daily lives. My au pair was indispensable to the family and birthing babies seemed to be my mother's forte. She had girls and boys and would sometimes forget our names.

She likes to dawn fur coats and attends military galas as much as she liked visiting relatives in the slums of Brooklyn. Her taste for suburbia was not an acquired taste but a lifestyle that was forced upon her by her husband a once divorcee'. She missed the best parts of her youth and instead of a young twenty something she was the middle-aged homemaker that appeared to be as adept at cooking, cleaning, and folding clothes as Martha Stewart. As soon as her husband left for work she would begin her daily regimen of chores and she sewed numerous dresses and pants. The first part of her day went smoothly and she nursed her babies and put them down for a nap. When she thought that all of her children were sleeping she put on some Marvin Gaye and swayed silently to the music. I would enjoy learning the Watusi and the Jerk as she would transition from one record to the next. This was the closest that I ever got to my mother. We moved constantly and the activities that my father became involved with were becoming highly politicized in the media. Finally, we were relocated to a very remote location which greatly displeased my mother as she enjoyed taking frequent trips to New York to visit her drug-crazed family.

Papa began to invest in real estate and plan for his retirement. Frequent trips to Mississippi and his alma mater were successful and they began to make plans to develop a University there. Papa had been the school Chaplain at an HBCU and during the 1960's was an advocate of the civil rights movement. He became close friends with a Renaissance author at a university in New England and along these lines he met my mother, a young student. Her younger sister had ambitions of becoming an attorney and attended a prestigious Ivy League school while mother grew old nursing babies. She was envious of her younger sister and watched while she lived her dreams of being a wealthy, jet-setting debutante who attended fashion week in Milan, Italy. Mother knew that Papa's health was failing and she would not be able to take care of all of the children, so she began to make plans to move to Mississippi with his family. During her time in the city she had plastic surgery and changed her name. The southern lifestyle did not lend itself to such extravagant things and she began to forsake her married life. She became the woman I loathed with her new mate that she vacationed with in Atlanta and the Bahamas. We began to wonder when we would ever see this woman again. My father patiently waited for her to return and instead of alerting authorities assumed the responsibilities of child-rearing as well as you could expect from a man of his age. The eldest sibling began to manage much of these obligations and there was much whispering about the nature of the child's relationship to her paternal father. These rumors were simply based upon lies and innuendo of the town's folks because there were some people that were inbred cousins. But, the love Papa had for his children been the love of a grandparent and many who knew him were treated that way. Mother was often left behind during summer vacations to Mississippi and the aunts, uncles, and cousins made the children feel welcome and loved.   With the big city far away the gulf life was tedious and burdensome. Picking peas, planting crops, milking cows, and harvesting eggs was done by the noonday. All of the people on the farm worked together so that they could eat. The nearest neighbors were so far that you could only reach them by telephone. The family had a small farm located a few miles from the main home and some of the uncles would stay in a small shanty there while we visited. Those summers were hot and shoes were never worn unless we dressed for something "fancy' like going into town for church. Most of the church members had their own farms and were distant cousins as well. They recalled tales of how the church was one of their first schools.

The grass roots campaign to build a university began during these talks as word spread of the 'preacher boy' who made it in the big city. The other church leaders had returned to help their small town recuperate from its economic losses and to bring new blood to the dwindling town.   Small towns are quiet and people know each other. Family values are placed as a high priority and neighbors are treated like family. Papa eventually decided to retire and purchased a home next to a successful lawyer. His family embraced the young children as their own. Mother

chose to leave him for the other man and that was fine as long as the children were

allowed to visit often.

At first, she made a big deal about taking the houses and demanded that he paid the bills, bought her cars, and gave her money. When he would come to check on the family she filed restraining orders. It was a very public ordeal and a most embarrassing one especially, when he refused to pay and she had to apply for welfare. The light bill or water bill sometimes went unpaid for months. Our school clothes were meager as were our meals. Many times we starved. One of my siblings became promiscuous and was mean as the dickens. She would fight and was popular with the boys. I struggled in school to make good grades and the teachers rewarded my efforts. Mother began to be resentful of the extra attention and she was not able to afford lunch so I went hungry.

Children were wealthy at my new school and they noticed that I had a peculiar smell. They also noticed how good my grades were and while they were not particularly rude they did not want to make friends with me either. Mother worked and did not spend time with us. I was bullied every day by my older sibling but she never took notice. I had very heavy menses and clotting but she never took me to the doctor, medical bills were too expensive. During my early childhood years I'd had surgery on my esophagus and I can remember being sickly but as I got older dad taught me how to play sports.

In general, the family life was normal and the school year continued on with little mishaps. I missed Papa every day and would inquire about him often. Over the years we became accustomed to his long absences. As the permanency of the separation from him became evident to me I became more inquisitive about

June. June appeared to have little interest in being a father to me unless I rejected Papa and called him 'Dad'. This was not a problem for the other siblings primarily because they were to young to have any profound memory of Papa. The maternal and paternal bond was not there. I did not want to express something that I was not feeling. Nor did I think that Mother's indiscretions should continue to reek havoc on my conscience. I wanted solidarity. The ability to choose my relationships and friends. She was happy with June and that was her prerogative. Most people would understand such a change is normal. He began to become moody and persistently question me concerning my daily activities. I resented his presence in my life and felt that the relationship was doomed from the beginning. Having him around did not make my life easier but it made it harder. Papa was upset and distrustful of all of us now. The light bill would sometimes go unpaid. I was not given money for lunch and dinner meals were paltry. He was not the only reason for my suffering and to further complicate matters, Mother was searching for a job in law enforcement.

I played soccer, softball, and even baseball. I was the only girl on our minor league team but spending summers in the country I learned how to hit a ball. I never was much good at basketball but I enjoyed ballet and still good at gymnastics. So eventually, my classmates accepted me and voted my cheer captain for our field day. I won a trophy in the school wide run and it was the last time that I would experience any success in school. Private schools would write letters offering me academic scholarships and all were but rejected by my family. Due to the drab clothes and the skipped lunches they determined that I would qualify for state funded tutoring which was to take place in an institution.

Eventually, I earned the scholarship back but by now my parents relationship was near divorce again. Mother sent me to Ohio to live with family. I was happy for the first time in a long time. I ate a lot and we were almost a family. Mother began to say that she needed me to return home so that she could get her child support so I was sent back to Mississippi. She was so elated when I got home but she was angry to discover that my cousin and I had written rap songs and I learned to be a hip hop dancer. She started an argument and threatened to kill me with a butcher knife. My cousin was still in high school and had come out to his family as *gay*, but he wanted to be a hairdresser and transgender. My cousins were the same age as my siblings and living with a transgender taught me to be patient and accepting of cultural differences.

For instance, he still had a girlfriend so the thought of him being transgender for him meant that he would only be seen as a gay man and not treated as a woman which is what he desired. Finally, the argument ended in my mother attempting suicide *again* by taking pain medication. The threat of exposure of this dreadful secret would be potentially devastating to the family, so this was kept behind closed doors. My stepfather was eventually able to persuade her to come back to her senses. She never attempted suicide again as far as I know but over the next few years the drama only worsened and they later divorced.

There are differing accounts of what took place over the next few years but it began with a classmate that was distributing an album for a local act. The act had no name and they were called the 'rebels' because they came from families of crack addicts. When mother found out that I had befriended these people she placed me in a rehab facility and although I never tested positive for drugs they offered me additional counseling instead. Mother never came to visit me and alternated between visits here and jail until I returned home to Papa. The community knew that family life was not so great and I would often be invited to spend the night or get a free meal. Mother resented me for wanting to leave and live with Papa so she disowned me by not allowing me to live with her at home. I drew closer to my friends and worked several jobs to support myself it was still hard. Dancing, singing, and rapping with these small groups only earned enough for me to eat or sleep for maybe a week at a time.

Drugs and gangs were beginning to pervade even our suburban town so I wasn't inclined to hang out with the rap groups and enrolled in college. By this time our sheriff had begun selling narcotics and prostitution so the town was becoming overwhelmed by vigilantes. It was around this time that I was hospitalized and went into a coma for two weeks. When I awoke I could not walk or even feed myself. The police reported that I had been stabbed by my sister and another boasted that I had been shot. I had amnesia and was addicted to pain killers. The differing stories are a source of great speculation and there are not differing witness accounts. Over the years my health dwindled but I continued to work and achieve my goal of graduating college.

One of my friends from the Mississippi town where I grew up with my father moved to the city to live with me. Later, we were married and he began to develop his talent as a sports editor. Fame and success were to follow as were more family drama. The murder of a local drug addict would turn my whole world topsy-turvy and I was soon to discover the secret truths about my father and his roots that changed my life for good.

The tougher the road and the harder the journey, the more difficult it can become to endure. Life will have many challenges but only the strong will survive. I am a survivor and it will help me to tell my story in my own words. For the generation to come to have an opportunity to learn from my struggles is an obligation that I feel I have met by writing this book.

The ongoing strife between my parents ultimately led to their separation. Along with the downward spiral of their relationship went Papa's political goals as mother sought fervently to end his career through public slander. My sister began to run away at during this difficult time which caused my parents to argue even further. Police would show up at our home with the youngster in tow claiming that she had been found by local store owner a half mile from our home.

Our new home in the south was a child's playground equipped with a swimming pool. The neighbors were middle-aged Caucasian that resented African American's but greeted us with civility. It forged a unique bond between my siblings and me as race became a dominating factor in our social setting. Papa was a mixed breed son of immigrants that owned farm land in the country and he was quite proud of his heritage, boasting about it often. He told us of how he earned his freedom from slavery because of his genealogical background and cautioned us about the heavy handed slave master because this was the only law that he knew. I became weary of hearing such tales and mother often belittled him publicly calling him 'dumb' because he still feared the white man. Although, I was petrified at the thought of being lynched it was not an intrinsic part of our culture during the latter part of the twentieth century. Papa was an old relic and I cherished my relationship with him dearly because I realized how lonely and alone he felt. This relationship often brought spite and resentment from mother as she fought for her freedom from this tyrant.

I often pitied Papa when he told me about life in the south during his youth. Surprisingly, my eyes would dampen as my heart sunk knowing that he may not be alive to experience my life's journeys with me. The commitment that he had to his family and parishioners was unabated as he continued to travel the world spreading the Gospel. He took an avid interest in hunting and fishing but, enjoyed watching television. Sports and the news were the only programs that captivated him. He would stare rapturously at the set explaining in vivid details the history of the sport or the President's private thoughts on the matter. I listened as my mind assimilated the new knowledge which I would share with my classmates.

Teachers challenged me more because I was African-American and they often assumed that I would not learn as easily as the rest of the students. My sister was a big help to me until she began to runaway. Before this happened I would deliver flowers for a local florist and get paid bi-weekly. People were proud to say that I was working to help my oversized family which we sometimes took for granted. I began to realize that mother was taking the money that I earned and spending it Papa was always angry with mother for spending too much money on clothes. She believed in Reagonomics and the promises he made of wealth and prosperity. Papa's meager earnings dwindled as mother made massive purchases from upscale New York boutiques and expensive interior upgrades. She soon became bored with that and began proceedings for a divorce. As the arguments became more heated my sister ran away more frequently. Allegations of child abuse were running rampant and mother began taking pictures after corporal punishments were administered. A major blowup was recorded on a cleverly placed tape deck and the final letters were mailed to the home. Friends arrived from Tennessee to help mother move and we were to start our new school the following day. Papa was distraught and he appeared to be man burdened with the guilt of losing his wife and children.

Life in the new school was strange because outside of a military setting there were no 'rules' or moral guidelines. Civilians may not seem to have an ethical value system when certain moral laws are not actively enforced. Military is formal and strict and civilians are lax and free to do as they wish. Moreover, when the punishment is removed behaviors must be adapting to acclimate to the new setting. Children ogled at us as if we were from another planet and I felt like a specimen being examined underneath a microscope. Once adjustments were made teachers began to accommodate my learning styles and quickly found that there was an alternative means of an education available to me. Mother was not willing to permit the changes to be made unless I was accompanied by my younger siblings.

I would now begin a three hour journey to school at 5 o'clock a.m. every weekday. Sometimes the neighborhood children would come over but mother strictly forbade us to have guests in the home.

Church was still an important part of our lives as mother began to refer to herself as a minister and dated several members of the congregation. She was unwilling to relinquish the title of importance that she held while married to Papa and continued to misrepresent her. Over the next decade she would slowly turn into a pariah in the suburbs where she lived. She had found a job working for a local newspaper plant and met a young street hustler named June. June had six children and still lived at home with his mama. June was mother's new male friend that had moved in with us last month. When Papa came to pick us up for visitation mother called the police and filed a restraining order. June was so angry that he threatened mother if she did not stop him from coming around. The neighbors had called police after witnessing an altercation between June and Papa but we were not home. Mother had demanded child support during the separation but Papa was still in love with the woman he married twenty years before. June flew into a jealous rage and the children were casualties in their love/hate relationship.

At dinner Mother announced her plans to marry June. Despite the elegance of the meal and its guests, words of hatred spewed forth from my mouth. My hands shook and my heart raced as I tried to control the venomous rage. Mother stared at me and it meant that a beating was to follow. The beatings had become an everyday occurrence from the time before the divorce. At eleven years-old I had decided that it was time for me to take a stance and I still wanted to have a relationship with my real father. Marrying June meant that the relationship with Papa would come to an abrupt end. The next year my menses would start along with heavy cramping but, the clotting gave rise to fear. Mother was not the type to turn the advent of my menses into an occasion to be recognized so she was very blaze when I mentioned my problem with clotting. As she sat before the fan and watched television my siblings gathered around her legs, she continued to pull the comb through her child's hair. Bare utterances were perceptible from her lips as a ventriloquist is fond of his dummies so is she of her favorite pet. I was once again shunned by the family and sent away to my room.

African cultures send the women out of the village during the time of menstruation. They consider the menstrual women to be a curse. I prayed a shallow prayer hoping that my mother would take heed to my warning before the conditioned worsened. My eldest sibling was the only one who showed a response which is as much as could be expected. As usual, mother ordered her to speak and she did but mother never glanced in my direction. Surely, if I approached her I would be quickly recoiled by a hard slap to face and maybe even pummeled to the floor. My siblings would cower in a corner, their faces covered in shock and horror hoping that they wouldn't be next. Mother bragged about her abusive tactics to anyone within earshot stating that if you mess with her you would be 'sorry'.

I was also 'banned' to the basement in a room once occupied by a teenager who was the child of a family friend. I shared the small basement apartment with another sibling and a door opened up to the veranda which led out to a small pond and vineyard. Her favorite was spared the humility of suffering such indecencies of living in a dingy, must dwelling. I quickly adjusted to the dank, dark, dungeon as I began to scour her private documents that were stored there. Once discovering a death certificate for a relative that cited AIDS related pneumonia for cause of death. I wondered had she considered their lifestyle choices when making those frequent visits to New York. I confronted her with the knowledge of the relatives passing. She cursed me to the day of my birth. It was then that the relationship between mother and I became irreparable.

Papa lived in a small community in southern Mississippi close to the New Orleans. He lived amongst lawyers and social workers yet there were those who cared enough to protect his children and we called them 'aunty'. Our 'aunties' loved us unconditionally but they disapproved of mother's strict discipline and would voice their concerns. As the days grew longer and colder I knew that fall would soon be upon us and we would be returned home to mother and June. June never spoke much and worked late hours. He was the brooding sort. His muscular build was infamously associated with his personality and as such he garnered fame. The couple appeared to be content and June would soon begin community college. Mother never complained when June was around. She always taught us the way to please a man was through his stomach. She would cook him large meals and spare us whatever meat was leftover from those meals. We fought mercilessly to prevent hunger but it was no use.

I planned to spend the weekend with a classmate with the promise that the family would order pizza. My classmate and slept-over before but mother was moody so I crept to her house after school. Mother notified local authorities and threatened to press charges against the family that allowed me to spend the night. She followed through with the threat by placing me in counseling indefinitely. The family was embarrassed by the scandal but continued to have communications with me throughout the ordeal. Most notably mother was once friends with the woman and the two would style their hair the same. Mother would soon become prone to more erratic behavior prompting a call by school officials to social services. Mother blamed me for the disruptions and decided that I should be placed in an orphanage. The mere prospect of separating from the family caused me severe anxiety. Papa would later research the orphanage and come to visit me disguised as a church worker.

The day Papa arrived I was in a fog of under heavy sedation. Doctors medicated us daily so that we were zombies trained to eat, talk, and sleep. Papa held his finger to his lips prompting me to silence as he motioned to the clerk to permit him access to the premises. He gave no indication that he was my father but told them that he was a local minister. He asked me how long I had been in the facility and instructed me not to tell Mother of his arrival to the city because she would be none the wiser. Mother had maliciously and contemptuously denied Papa access to the hospital. I questioned her judgments concerning her decisions not to allow Papa to see me during this time. Certainly, her co-workers considered her a hard-working dedicated that spent hours preparing church services each Sunday. Friends and neighbors were also lied to about my whereabouts as speculation mounted. The hideous secret would be permanently hidden while the family prepared for my return home by moving yet again.

Papa said that while visiting me he had an opportunity to address the director of the hospital and that he was able to persuade him to negotiate my release. Papa did not visit the new home until the relationship between him and June was repaired. June was a project manager and raking in loads of money from the new economic boom. He no longer resented Papa although; I would remind him that my child support donations were used to pay his college loans. Nobody noticed when I returned home because the new move also meant attending a new school. One of my siblings took me school shopping in our old neighborhood to hush the wagging tongues of the people.

Before I was institutionalized my classmates had nominated my for classroom representative and the gorgeous quarterback on the football team flirted with me daily. Teachers noticed bruising and swelling but never spoke to me about it. One day my mother and sister picked me up from school and she brought a belt. She beat me in the school hallways shouting obscenities. When we arrived home she told me to pack an overnight bag and they conjured up stories of egregious acts that I had committed. She never mentioned how my sister had shoved a friend through a siding glass door nearly severing an artery. Or how one sibling had attacked another with a knife causing injury to the upper cavity. But it was the unneeded attention that I was getting at school that she resented me for and indicated the new state legislation (education) gave her the right to make the decision.

While most preteens and adolescence were developing in a normal environment I was locked away with druggies and mentally retarded students. The talks were not productive because as I began to talk about my home life Mother would dispute anything that I said that was negative about her. I endured hours of family sessions where she would dramatize her life attempting to generate animus towards me from my siblings. My physical appearance became neglected and my hair was notoriously unkempt. The proper tools were not provided to me by my family at this time so eventually staff would supplement the hair equipment. Staff would take me on personal outings to allow me an opportunity to eat and dine in a real restaurant. I had dreams of leaving this place and how my life would be when I left. Weekend visits were successful but once I returned home Mother had new plans for me.

She had planned to ship me away to live with relatives in Ohio and there began my journey into adulthood. My family was still closely bonded subsequent the divorce but there was resentment and bitterness that seemed tangible during holidays or family gatherings. Mother had dreamed of living a virtuous life with a new husband but her dreams were never actualized as she began a down-ward spiral into mental instability. The instability impacted the family as she was prone to hallucinations. Abuse was her way of maintaining her control of the family unit. She threatened long term treatment facilities to anyone that dare report her to authorities. Silence was not an effective tool either since the hallucinations caused her to believe that she heard voices.

The modern age of technology at the advent of the internet had not yet yielded such inventions as the camera phones. Cellular phones were also a commodity. We owned one and each time I left I would take it with me. It had to be charged up using a car battery and/or wall adapter. If there were camera phones I would simultaneously download a video of the wild tantrums mother would have and upload it onto you tube for the world to see. She was infamous for using manipulative tactics when faced by accusers. Friends and family supported me throughout the ordeal and it would be decades before I was able to face myself in the mirror. Social workers and teachers have since taught me how to set goals and accomplish task. I am finally a part of society and treated as a human being. At one point in my life I was a caged animal willing to do anything to eat and find shelter. I had an inner desire to fight. Like a caged animal I was too afraid to trust my caretaker, Mother. When I thought that I had a good reason for abandoning home life and pursuing a stable home environment outside of my nuclear family, people said that I was wrong. The only people that I trusted were hundreds of miles away in a small bicoastal community in a rural town in south Mississippi. Worse yet, the city slick ways that Mother learned while visiting her ne'er do well kin in New York, were the skills that she had trained the children with to develop them into manipulative liars.

Papa was a strong and withstood public criticisms and speculations to embrace the vestiges of a ruined marriage. At one point mother's contemptuous accusations nearly cost him a twenty-year career due to his employer's stringent moral policies. His reputation was impeccable and the speculations were easily dismissed after a quiet transfer to a remote location outside of the United States. Through his offshore assignment he garnered more world renowned success by receiving accolades from a government ambassador for his educational and peace efforts of race relations. My life was near perfect but Mother's controlling domineering personality would not permit me the freedom to engage in a conversation with Papa unless she listened intently from another extension.

"The sins of the father would be revisited upon the children….cursing a

family tree for generations."

Time was of the essence and there was precious little time that was left for me in a home with a family torn apart by infidelity. The new school was full of bright intelligent and responsible teens. The youths had affluence and my new neighbors were an R&B powerhouse. Before I would wake up each morning I could hear the sputtering and revving of sports scooters outside my window. The young teen sensations would show off before us knowing that single women were occupied by the home. Mother was pleased and our happy lives were marred by the intermittent bitter wrangling that were interspersed between June and she. The fights were over money and the food pantry was sparse. The family was able to keep afloat when the older siblings obtained jobs at a local eatery. Mother never minced words and she demanded every penny of our earnings filing her tax returns claiming all children, working and not working, as dependent. While she still received monthly allocations of child support and both June and her worked full-time jobs. June's new job as a project manager paid him well and his lofty disposition was deeply resented by the younger siblings. He was the epitome of nepotism and it disgusted me greatly. Every meal was prepared for him and the rest of the family was forced to fend for them. Every dime of child support was paid towards his college education and transportation. He drove two cars and the spare vehicles were garaged not to be driven by Mother.

He was a man of few words but appeared to be extremely judgmental. His family that he lived with prior to the marriage were an intermingle of drug addicted single mothers and destitute single men. He had bore many children through numerous affairs with drug addicted women and insisted that he support each of them. The time that he spent between families would allow that he sometimes stayed away from home many nights. He preferred to live with the mobility of a single person but never neglected his financial obligations to the support and upkeep of the property. He worked tirelessly to prove his self worth, but to mother the separate bank accounts and the overnight stays were too much. They argued heatedly on one evening in particular. I had stayed home until this point but was prone to overnight visits with friends. I stood blocking the door so that he would not storm out of the home but he crushed me esophagus like a delicate flower. My five foot frames no match for his strength. Mother pleaded with him as he efficiently deflected her blows. He proceeded with his threat to my life while my body wilted in a heap the floor. Mother rushed to my side and he agilely stepped over my body shoving the door against me while he exited the home his anger piqued.

The frequent visits to Southern Mississippi were an escape from the hectic city life and tormentors family. It was hard to look Papa in the eye knowing the betrayal that Mother had brought upon him and we fought tirelessly while we visited him there. Aunty would tell us not to fight and she disciplined us accordingly. She also cautioned us about drugs, denouncing Mother's manipulative methods of averting justice by placing me in an intensive long-term program. I trusted and adored this woman. She had three small children and was divorced but she was the only Mother that we had because Papa rarely dated and had no intentions to remarry. After all he had single daughters and adored the 'broads' as he so fondly, referred to them. Aunties' son was a charming young boy that had a strange accent. It was the type of accent that you never heard in the South. It reminded me of some of the people that wore colorful clothing in New York when Mother took us for visits. They ate different food and spoke a different language. Man was like them but he was a southerner. Man Man was a young tyrant ordering me and the other girls to do his bidding. Although, he was probably younger than most of us he demanded this respect and he was well treated. He was active and a speed runner his secret was having club feet that enabled him to perform with the dexterity of a pro athlete. I competed against most boys and in High School would be trained alongside an Olympic Gold Medalist.

Man Man had natural talent. He reminded me that I was a girl and that he would not be beat by a girl. The only girl that was tough enough to stand up to he was his sister that towered over us all. She would poke him playfully in the chest. He was so proud that he would object and proceed to receive a beating. The silent whimpers would soon turn to war cries as he would endure the struggle with her indefinitely. Tears would come to my eyes, but he learned to be tough by enduring these beatings. His way of earning respect was by fighting. His playground theatrics would soon amount to huge success in the NBA. I had a time growing up around these two, but they had the love of family and that would be sure to stand the test of time. Nothing could separate the bond that had survived decades however; there would be some trying times.

These were the best of times and these were the worst of times. Mother struggled to raise her brood without any influence from Papa. He had a large influx of relatives that were a short distance away. Papa's family managed to get together every year for family reunions and folks would come from all over. The familial bond remained intact and stories of success became more and more forthcoming. His family lineage dated back to ancestral ties that were centuries old. Plantations were an intrinsic part of the southern culture. When the civil rights movement began it meant an end to the plantation life. Summers of my youth spent on the farms were not just recreational. Each meal had to be tilled by the hands of aging and retired men that had not earned a decent salary since the Vietnam War. Education was mistaken for neither uppity niggers so the affluence with which I had grown accustomed was neither accepted here nor commonplace. Fear of lynching years after the marching had taken place was on the heartbeat of every freed African American person that stayed in the South. There was a large group of relatives that transitioned into railroad jobs and traveled to the North. They had taken up residence in a mining community and started their own 'set' of Dixon's. Dixon was Papa's family name and he was quite proud of his mulatto mother and Creole grandmother.

Talks of his heritage often ended in a disgruntled gripe about genocide and race relations in America. As military servicemen, one of which came from a long line of military servicemen, he had undergone training into sensitive military operations. His grandfather owned a large plantation and still farmed diligently with the help of his large family. The twenty or so siblings that he shared also had small herds so that the farm extended ups the hillside and over into the next city limits. The expansion of the railroad meant new developments and it also meant that wealthy billionaires such as the Carnegies and the Rockefellers would be utilizing it for business purposes. The longest standing director of the railroad was a distant cousin to Papa's grandfather and true to legend the name held power and notoriety in the South. Papa used his biracial ethnicity and heritage to garner political favor amongst the ethnic demographic. He was a man of impeccable character that suffered great indignities at the hands of his white superior officers. Yet, he served with the gratitude of civility humbled by his roots and empowered by the faith of his people.

Colored people were the largest demographic that populated the Southern regions. The lives of southern traditions were deeply embedded into the psyche of the people. Hard times meant that they would be ever mindful of the economy. The lifeblood of many was spent to preserve the vestiges of a sluggard economy. Papa was born during the Great Depression and he was a Southern Boy through and through. Strong willed and mean as a 'rattlesnake' he got tough by fighting with his brothers. The men mated as they primal instincts led them to and fighting was a way to improve stamina. The toughest was always the tallest and 'talking tall' was a way to describe a braggart. 'Fighting words' was law in the south. The way of men would be sure to change because with the new railroad brought jobs and educational advancements. Country colored folks would farm and hunt for food. Guns were needed for protection while hunting was a necessary part of survival. If you killed you ate it whether it was in the woods or a lake. Mother was the chef and could make anything taste worth eating.

Hunger was akin to stress which it brought on for many men that struggled to feed the growing families. Spirits soothed the souls of overworked and under compensated workers. Corn liquor was ciphered off by more backwoods folks and was enjoyed secretly. Men would emerge from the woods inebriated as well as full of jokes and laughter. This was a time of fellowship and bonding amongst the men folks. The scarcity of liquor and guns contributed to the neglible manner in which homes were kept. Doors were not commonplace and were much of a nuisance. Although, one could not overlook the obvious fact that animals were equally as comfortable inside of a homestead as outside. Chickens would run across the barren floors. We enjoyed having them as pets. We enjoyed the eggs and the meals that we cooked on the farm. We got along so well that poverty was not a burden but, through hard work and determination we could achieve success. Papa saved his earning. He was once duped by a relative who squandered away his savings. He began to shrewdly save so that this person, nor anyone else for that matter, would take him for granted again.

A church/school existed on the farm. The family gathered there every Sunday. We shared communions, baptisms, and Confirmation classes. We held Easter and Christmas Pageants. Thanksgiving style meals were sometimes prepared by the older women of the church. Everybody had relatives in this church and was my family through Papa's bloodlines. Before the divorce, Mother disliked visiting the farm. My parents would travel any distance to vacation there during the summer. The trips were long but we drove a new minivan that made the trip enjoyable. We stopped only for restroom breaks and to site see. Each town that we traveled through was different. The United States countryside was beautiful from the backseat of a station wagon. My bones would get stiff and tired. There were short stops along the trip so that we could stretch our legs. After the divorce, Papa had help driving from his older children and we still took the long trips. We would sing songs. We would doodle, crossword puzzles. We would also play sight games to pass the time during these long vacation rides cross-country. Papa knew a lot of people. He often stopped and visited with friends and family during our frequent journeys to the South. If we could not be accommodated elsewhere, we lodged in low class motels. Mother would protest this, by morning we would awake to find her defiantly slumbering in the car. Sometimes at night these types of motels/hotels would be long-term residences of prostitutes and druggies. Later, when I enrolled at City College I would find myself embroiled with a bitter battle between myself and family. The prospect of living in one of these types of places was imminent. I was ever mindful of Mother's defiant stance. I vowed to work at more than one place of employment to avert the dangers that would surely allow for me to make a slum ghetto my permanent home. Papa's love for me spared me of this unfaithful demise. In doing so the course of my life would be changed forever.

I have oftentimes wondered what my life would have been like had my parents not divorced. Now I don't do that anymore. It is not relevant to me the doings of others. Partly because after the murder I began to recognize the ugly truth about myself and maternal family.

"And those he predestined, he also called; those he called,

he also justified; those he justified, he also glorified."

Romans 8:30

There is an inner strength within us all that grants us the desire to become successful. For some success may mean a new car, house, college degree. Success is fleeting to others and yet others do not equate monetary value with happiness or success. The degree to which an individual desires to achieve a normal life can be considered success. The greatest accomplishment that I made happened to be my own floundering attempt at success. I mothered a child, through deception concealed the child's birth. Having been too ashamed to admit to Papa that I had unlawfully conceived. The public embarrassment and shame that would bring to my family was too much to bear. Secretly, I withheld my small bundle of joy. When the realization came that my secret had been exposed I was emotionally ready to accept the rejection from Mother. Papa was very disappointed blaming me as if I were the only one responsible for the child. Later, it brought upon me a determination to follow through with my education.

Papa expressed to me his contempt from a biblical standpoint. Whereas, I sometimes felt the fire and brimstone sermon was overwhelming it also made me angry? Did God think that I should be rejected for my sin? Was the underlying infallibility of a person with expectations of perfection behind Papa's angst? Whilst I would discover the Bible and reread nearly the entire book. I remember several times over the years of being funneled through the governmental red tape and now developed a keen sense of self awareness.

Mother was domineering and judgmental. She made a big show of her anger by charging at me. She hurled her body across the entire length of the living room in seconds as she taunted me with her heavy New York accent lingering. She would always boast to us about her toughness as a street girl that did not tolerate nonsense from anyone. She continued to follow through with her threats and was unabated by anyone who was present at the time. Mother firmly planted her foot squarely in between my legs. Underneath her breath she let out an 'humph' while extending her leg before her. I could feel the heaviness of her foot as it slammed into my secret place. My vulnerability brought me crumpled into a heap on the floor. She shouted obscenities which were completely discernable to me. I felt a sharp pain and then shock. I coughed from my chest and ran into the nearby bathroom locking the door behind me. I could hear my sibling demand her to stop and threaten that she would make me report this to law enforcement. My fear from my mother had waned to the point where I even consider doing this, but of course I would have nowhere to live. My cousin told me to leave with her that day and I would not return to Mother's home again.

There were times in my life when uncertainty was a sure sign that trouble lie ahead. Now I have the peace of God which surpasses all understanding. The Lord has a plan for each of us. My struggles were a part of God's masterful plan for my life. Some would say that you are lucky. I believe that blessing come from the Lord. He says that Lo I will be with you always even until the end of the earth. When you are staring eye to eye with a murderer, pray for mercy. When you are homeless and out of money, call for help. But when you are abandoned by every living relative where do you find the strength to move forward. Drugs are an easy way out for most people in that situation. They ease the pain of an emotional hell that torments you night and day. Drugs can cause many pitfalls and snares in your life. Surrounding yourself with positive people can be a help when you are struggling through addiction. David wrote the book of Psalms. He said that the Lord is a fortress and he looks to the hills from whence cometh his strength. David was a man that had lusted after another man's wife. His adultery led to him committing a fateful error which also caused the death of this man. The David that slew Goliath had also fallen from grace because of his fleshly desires. Men would openly lust after me and I would sometimes take advantage of their generosity. By accepting these favors I was allowing myself to sink further and deeper into the mire of sin. It made Mother feel that her daughter was of some value to her. She warned me about the Pimps and hustlers that took advantage of women. She told me never to let a man use me and to not sleep with a man that did not want to marry me. She told me not to accept favors from anyone and to work for whatever I earned.

I would sometimes feel jealous of women that had beautiful children and handsome husbands. My envy led me to sin with men that were not my husbands. I would outwardly portray myself as a woman that enjoyed being treated to the finer things in life. Yet, I struggled harder than most women my age. By the time that I was seventeen I was working double shifts and had a public commentary on the radio. I enjoyed the attention from men that came to see me perform at shows. The feeling of my feminine prowess was power and it helped me to maintain my focus. I had dreams of becoming a successful party promoter and one day joining the staff for the radio station where I called in for daily commentary sessions. The deejay and I would stay up chatting into the early hours of the morning when I finished my shift. If I was lucky I would pull a double. My adrenaline could keep me up for hours. I didn't need drugs to stay awake but, when I slept I could sleep forever.

The community began to embrace this movement of young and upcoming entrepreneurs. My friends even made a rap video commenting on me new way of dress and joking about the psychiatric therapy that Mother insisted that I needed to purge the raunchy music from my psyche. She said that I was sinning and needed Jesus. She had me baptized into a new faith. Anytime that she felt that I needed to be 'redeemed' she would arrange for the Pastor to baptize me again. Unlike my cohorts, I attended church faithfully. Soon that meant leaving those weekend excursions behind. Every local act called upon my dance crew to perform and we sometimes got paid.   Of course there were the comps and we gained notoriety. We promised to clean up the lyrics to the songs and would only perform clean acts. The dirty strippers would sometimes try to break up the movement but, we were by nature converted Christians. The songs began to reflect our commonalities. While some began to dope up we continued to support each other emotionally. The money was low and the effort was becoming a movement. One radio deejay decided that he would dedicate a new station that only played the music which we wanted to listen to. Sin city became a new Southern town. People came from all over to celebrate spring break. They would tear the down the walls of segregation and break every law known to man. Video cameras recording the publics' trust in it's local government waned as average citizens were unwitting participants in the month long affair.   A person would leave fifteen minutes early for work and be stuck in a long line of late night partiers. The lines turned into two hour long grid-lock traffic. The intermingling of rush hour workers and drunken partiers was a new phenomenon. The party goers would disrobe publicly and dance on top of cars while music blared from subwoofers hooked up to powerful amplifiers. The loud noise could be heard from several yards away. Bootleggers would distribute music tapes and pornographic material. They would sell merchandise from nearby retail establishments that had been recently looted. Curious onlookers would become new victims of robbery or rape. The crowd would envelope the women shouting for them to remove their clothing. The women would not comply and attempt to walk away. The crowd quickly swelled to twenty or thirty men that chanted to the women to strip naked as the forced her to perform sex acts in public. There was little that law enforcement could do to control the crowds and the rampant drug activity. Marijuana and other drugs were used with disregard to the laws. This was Woodstock of the twentieth century. What happened in Sin City stayed in Sin City?

After a month long of the terrible looting finally the peace breakers would leave and the city would return to normal. The police would arrest some of the rioting party goers but, the problem had far reaching implications into how the city government was to operate.

The city was undergoing a major reconstruction overhaul in preparation for the upcoming Olympic Games. I had begun working as a computer science engineer by enrolling in a prestigious technology school which Papa agreed to pay for. He did not like the idea that I was on the fast track and had asked me to reconsider attending the school where he sat on the board of trustees. Although, I desired to be out from under the parental umbrella to experience life on my own terms. Friends that had graduated high school with me were persuasive when asking me to stay in town. Recently, I had

undergone a major operation.

" Behold, I am with you always, even unto the end of the earth."

Matthew 28:20

Today was a typical day and the pain in my abdomen had increased gradually until I became completely bedridden. My mother ignored this as she usually did because she had to work and nothing would keep her from doing her job. She had gained more important obligations through her employer when she tried to force me through the IDEA program and legislation. Superintendents and principals were fired as Mother continued to challenge local school officials regarding my education. At home she would criticize me saying that I was just like my father whom she detested. It was difficult for me to relate to people like her from an inner city. The bond that I'd forged with my friends in Mississippi was by doing what came natural to me and was an offense to her.

I was not retarded by any means, my test scores were outstanding. She noted that the law would not permit me to make any future strides in my education because she could not afford private schooling. The places that the insurance paid to get the private tutoring and counseling was not the typical places that people would send their children unless they needed help. Moreover, people began to publicly accuse Mother of child abuse a fact that she would deny until she was face to face with a judge and being charged with aggravated domestic battery.

The neighbors could hear her scream and yell at all hours of the night. The nearest service station had a pay phone and when I could get away, I would call a friend and ask permission to stay over for a night or two. Mother was from a time when abortion was illegal and she resented Papa saying that he forced her to have too many unwanted pregnancies. People were hesitant to comment on the private matters that took place behind closed doors. Rarely would the neighbors address the situation unless it was totally out of hand. Typically, calls to law enforcement were ignored and others would just mind their own business. Mother was not able to conceal the night when I was almost brutally murdered and one of my siblings was eventually charged.

My quick reflexes prevented the knife from further penetration. I tried to escape with my life my arm was numb and bleeding. Adrenaline and fear were the only emotions that I felt. I lay still and motionless on the floor as one of my siblings' screamed bloody murder. I could hear mother's calm calculating voice advising people to remain calm and she would handle it. I was covered by a sheet and I knew at this point that they thought that I was dead. As mother took my sibling from the room and calmly asked her to hand over the knife she assuaged her with words of reassurance. This was the most infuriating trait that Mother had. At this time, I was expecting the sheet to pull back and the violent assailant would attack me again. HHowever, when they left the room I calmly ran out of the nearest exit and patiently followed a narrow trek to the nearest store. The store clerk recognized me and stared in shock and disbelief as I related to them several times what had happened. With surprising efficiency the telephone dialer requested towels and dialed 911. The staff did not scream but had an eerie calm as if they expected the employee to follow through with her threats to harm me as she had done. The sibling that was employed there had been in several altercations with neighborhood girls and was bused to a school in the old neighborhood area because she felt more comfortable there.

They tried to calm me and shock began to wane as I realized that they were asking me what I was going to do about this situation. My future outlook on life was grim. They reassured me that I would be physically healed but that the emotional scars would remain with them all forever. My wounded body was crumpled in a heap on the floor of a convenience store and Mother would discover that was there. The store clerk called her home when I explained that the family member stabbed me she was in shock and disbelief. She thought that I was delirious and I listened intently to her explain to the woman that had just tried to kill me where I was. I could hear Mother shocked scream from the receiver as he motioned to reassure me that I would be okay. I vehemently shook my head and he held a hand over the receiver while he explained to Mother that I was trying to talk. When Mother pulled up the store clerk explained that an ambulance was in route. Mother suggested that she would take me to the hospital to expedite the process. The shocked store clerk heard distention in Mother's voice and tried to calmly explain to her why she should wait. Mother rushed me to the car declaring a state of emergency. The store clerk shook his head in complete bewilderment.

The ride to the hospital was punctuated by a deathly silence then, I inquired of Mother where we were going. The sibling that had committed the offense was in the car with me. Every child has an inner sanctum of innocence that only allows them to feel complete trust of people, especially loved ones. I felt violated and defiled yet, I trusted Mother when she said that she was taking me to a hospital. She drove for an hour, we had not visited a police station or a hospital while panic crept up through my veins. It had started at the base of my spine and nudged me in the shoulder. I hollered in pain but, Mother continued to drive. My sister told me to shut up and Mother drove obediently. My sibling told me that I was exaggerating that Mother had given me aspirin and to shut up.

I wondered if they were going to leave me in the dense heavily wooded area by which we traveled but, I dare not suggest it. When we arrived at a rural country hospital the emergency room was smaller than the interior of my home and there were curtains

dividing each individual bed. The country doctors asked me to explain my injuries so that

they would know how to respond. As I explained to the doctor how I had been impelled

by a large kitchen knife his face contorted into a mask of utter disbelief. He asked my

mother to step out of the emergency while he treated me and privately called law

enforcement. A nurse confirmed my story and apologized on my sibling behalf. They told

me that the pain medication would be a localized anesthetic. The pain medicine needed to

be repeatedly administered while the doctor worked quickly to repair the gaping wound.

He showed the nurse the layers of muscle that had been damaged during the attack. Next,

he explained to me that I would have to talk with the authorities. Mother was objecting to

an interrogation in the hallway while my sibling was shedding bitter tears.

Mother accused me of lying and the authorities explained that someone was going

to be taken to jail. The pity of the officers was evident and they were inclined to side with

Mother although they new that she was fabricating her story. The officer abruptly

handcuffed the person that attacked me and carted them away in a police cruiser. Mother

took me home in tears about what had happened. As I lay unconscious in the bed from

heavy pain medications, Mother arranged to have my sister released from jail. The events

that took place the next three days were baffling. Mother would take me to visit the

district attorney and they told her that she would have to lose custody of me. Mother

would not show any physical evidence to police of what happened and cleaned up the

mess by disposing of the knife.

Papa came to get me from the state's children's home and the nightmares would

never end. My stay with Papa was filled with arguments and tension. Papa knew that the knife had done more than just leave a physical scar, he took me to visit the doctor and they discovered the Cancer. Papa would allow me to stay home from school knowing that the cramping was crippling my body. Schoolmates would visit and Papa enjoyed having me there. He bought me a miniatures schnauzer that I named 'Fluffy'. Papa was still a hunting man and he never likened to having an animal in the house. When I became ill he made 'Fluffy' stay outside. Within a short time 'Fluffy' was like a wild beast and no amount of coaxing could change the pup that was once a housetrained purebred beast.

June who was suspiciously quiet throughout the whole ordeal did want the sibling that stabbed me to visit with Papa while I lived there. She came into town like a thief in the night. She was domineering and Papa told her the rules up front. We did not allow violence of any kind in our house; he was near tears when he spoke. He was persistent and demanded an answer for the deep betrayal that he felt by my sibling, she agreed to try to get along and before the summer she would be back to her old trifling ways.

Rotissa was a big mountainous woman. Her girth was twice the size a normal person and she only stood five feet six in height. My sister was after Rotissa's man and she would do anything to have him. She invited me to visit the boy at his family's ranch just a quarter mile west of where we lived. I hesitantly agreed after Papa insistently urged me to trust this child. As we approached the homestead Rotissa greeted us at the door with a huge welcoming smile. This was sure to change when my sister told me to ask for her husband. Rotissa charged out the door at me and I hurriedly explained that I was not the person she should be upset with. Rotissa came out onto the veranda and pointed an accusatory finger towards my sister. 'Oh you, I know who you are and I told you not to come around here.' What happened next was not at all what I had anticipated.   The two became heavily embroiled in a brawl on the front lawn. The men folk watched intently as blows were passed. I was body slammed on the ground like a sack of potatoes. I had neither the height nor girth of Rotissa and was by far the tiniest person involved in the altercation. I ran home and told Papa what was happening. We pulled around there in our pickup and my sister hopped in before anyone was hurt. She was not the victor but she held her own against Rotissa. The story was one of legends and would live on long after she had gone on to fame and success.

My sister stood a foot taller than I. When we were teens they labeled us Lil one and Big one. People would often see us and do a double take. The resemblance was uncanny. As youth I struggled to keep up with her. She was the mischievous sort and often would smile a deceptive grin when plotting her evil tactics. The children in our country club community were afraid of her. She would often challenge the young men to fist fights. Mothers of the young children would bring their maimed youths to our home and report to Mother what my sister had done. She used her gender as a way to excuse her behavior, but I often would be the mediator in situations such as these. Afraid that my presence was enough to implicate me as an agitator. The boys would say 'nigger' or worse and she would spit and kick.

Each year Mother and Papa held birthday parties in my honor and I would always get extravagant gifts. We did not have birthday parties for any of my siblings. My birthday was a time of celebration. My sister was a troublemaker and found a way to Bogart the toys before I could make good use of them. The entire community would come to these affairs. We had the time of our lives. I never argued with people that called me names and had an expansive vocabulary which I learned from my older siblings and Papa, the orator. This made it easier for the older children to take advantage of me at an impressionable   age. They would often teach me lyrics to rap. Because I took gymnastics they taught me to break dance as well. At the bus stop in the morning the older kids would encourage me to perform and clapped in adoration. The stress of being a younger sibling was becoming unbearable. I never shared with anyone the contempt that I felt for them. I knew that I was being exploited and the bullying was a source of entertainment to these tall sophisticated teenagers.

Mother would hire cheerleaders that babysat or the au pair would request one when she wanted a day off. The cheerleaders brought their boyfriends and they would make out in the 'fort' across the street. When I happened to witness them having sex on one occasion, I peed in my clothes. Mother demanded to know what happened from the cheerleader and she tried to stop the tears that rolled down my cheeks. Mother explained that I had peed in my clothing and that the cheerleader did not clean it up. Mother fired her and told her parents how the girl had gotten pregnant. I was hurt by this because I liked the cheerleader and she would teach me how to memorize high school cheers. I wanted to be a cheerleader just like her. I wanted to be popular with lots of boyfriends. I learned from her how to poise myself as a young girl. Quickly making friends with the neighborhood children and dismissing ones that I thought were to childish or disgusting like babies.

Michael Jackson released the *Thriller* album. MTV was in its infancy. Artists like Boy George were popular. Orphan Annie was aired on HBO. Mother prepared me breakfast in the mornings. I would watch MTV and soap operas. In the afternoons we folded clothes together. When she could employ an au pair she would. Jimmy Carter was the incumbent and Reagan was his adversary. This was the eighties and we were preppy suburbanites. Rabbits, mice, and the occasional snakes darted through our expansive yards. At night we would catch fireflies and watch them make sparkles inside of jars. The family members would come and visit from New York. Papa would take us to Busch Gardens and Kings Dominion. I joined the Girl Scouts. New York was a short distance from where we lived and the trip would take us up the coast. We frequented Washington

D.C.

City people were a different breed of character. They spoke differently and the behaved differently. Most importantly they dressed in wild colors, bandanas, and hairdo's. Wino's and homeless persons were a part of the landscape. The druggies and dealers were violent and gun violence was a part of our daily lives. Muggings and other crimes would take place daily.

My grandmother lived in a large brownstone in Brooklyn. Her home was approximately 3600 sq ft and dated back to the early turn of the century. The family had moved to the city when my grandfather sought employment at a firm. The children stayed with relatives while he worked to buy the new home. The family had grown in size and number. We gathered in the home during long breaks. There was room for every person on every floor. Mother had a large family but she did not know her extended family well. The men of the family were spiraling downward into drug abuse. Her brother overdosed on heroin and the others were definitely hooked. They would entertain prostitutes in our presence. This lifestyle was typical of any African American New York family, so I thought. It was certainly that way on my block. Our family had particular notoriety and my grandfather was the *mayor* of our block. With wealth and prosperity he made lavish expenditures. He drove a brand new Lincoln and it was clean.

My uncles frequented the casinos boasting of importance. Until the crack epidemic hit and then AIDS. My parents would share stories often in tears about the cancer that was spreading throughout our community. The neighborhood was overrun by drug addicts and criminals. Papa valued our suburban life even more so than the Big City. He insisted that we return to Mississippi to reestablish a bond with his family.

Throughout his military career he had gone on two world tours. He had become homesick. When he returned home he would come bearing gifts. He filled our heads with stories of exotic birds, animals, people, and places. He spoke many languages fluently. At night we would dream of the beautiful places and people that he had seen while there.

As our parents' friends were dying of the cancer. They began to expand the ministry to reflect lifestyles and embracing culture. The sixties struggles were behind them. The new technological age was upon us. But the cancer was killing people in the masses. Papa preached about homosexuality. It was not accepted in the military and many believed it to be the cause of cancer. Papa believed that people that were homosexual were not aware of it causing cancer. He believed that fornication and adultery were the causes of the cancer. Homosexuality was one aspect of the culture that people should be educated about. The other pastors in the ministry coordinated with him to develop training and workshops within the church to inform the public about AIDS awareness. This was unconventional at the time. Papa was a wise man and he knew that by spreading the word the public would be informed and   it help to assuage the fear or stigma associated with the terms: cancer, gay cancer, homosexual, AIDS. Soon my uncles wheel and dealing would lead to prison. He would succumb to complications from AIDS in the prison infirmary. Mother would get angry anytime you mentioned him but, she professed her love for her brother regardless of his faults.

Papa moved us to a small town similar to the one he grew up in Mississippi. Mother hated it. The kids at our new private school disliked our New York mannerisms and poked fun at us. The nuns expressed dissatisfaction with the idiosyncrancies which we had developed over our time spent in the Big City. I was formally trained into a

Catholic. I enjoyed Catholic school. The uniforms that we wore beget influence and prestige. Our home was in a modern middle class community where we were one of two families with in ground swimming pools. Papa would never allow those individuals to use it. During summer vacations they would crash the pool leaving empty beer cans in their wake. The home had a small solarium, Jacuzzi, and outdoor shower. There was a basketball court and a small creek.

Some of the boys in the neighborhood rode skateboards and built ramps. Mother purchased a skate board and I began to learn to do tricks on the board and my bicycle. I was above average in academics and athletics. I played soccer, baseball, and softball. I took ballet and jazz lessons and even participated in several talent competitions. I entered an oratory talent and did well enough to become a special feature. I enjoyed being in the lime light whether it was for singing, sports, or a class project that I entered into a science fair. I saw how success could be made at an early age. I became responsible for a local paper route. People knew me and I was finally able to distinguish an identity separate from that of my siblings. Sports were physically and emotionally challenging. The support of my friends and classmates help to make winning worthwhile. Competing was equally as relevant as participating in the sport. Developing athleticism was not an easy feat. Gymnastics enabled me to be limber. Pilates and yoga were strengthening my muscle tone and structure. I would bend my feet behind my head and walk around like a pretzel to entertain my family. I still practiced back flips and developed a break dancing routine.

While watching a Will Smith video I spun on my head. Mother cautioned me that I could break my neck. She hated rap and said that it was the devil's music. The *Parents*

Just Don't Understand video looked like an animated cartoon acted out by grownups. Mother stated how obvious it was that the rapper wanted to persuade youths to rebel. She was offended by the lyrics and opposed to the content of the videos. She saw a startling trend in the new music that was being presented. Michael Jackson's *Thriller* video was still popular, Prince released *Purple Rain*, and Whitney Houston was on the horizon. Christie Brinkley and Phil Collins were mainstream successes. Patrick Swayze released *Dirty Dancing*. Such was the culture of the late eighties. Except in this small town nobody wore legwarmers and colored hair. We wore fancy belts and oversized shirts or jellies. Town's folks stared at the strange dress of the trendy New Yorkers as if we were from another planet. Jeri curls were becoming more popular and each member of our family sported one. Cyndi Lau per rivaled Madonna for number one on the Billboard charts and it was easy to ignore the social degenerates that were contributing to the drug epidemic. Papa would no longer allowed frequent excursions to the Big City because of the unnecessary problems that were caused by being there and the violence. He censored every word we heard, book, music, radio. The house was Christian censored and child friendly. He was military but he did not use the defamatory language that precluded the euphemism 'to curse like a sailor.'

We played in our respective sports. My older sister was good at basketball and I at everything else except basketball. I was the worst basketball player known to humankind. In the game of soccer my coach would teach me how to be a star and the whole brood would come to see me shine. I had speed and ability which were a viable entity on the field. Children would stare in awe as I shot past them like a light. I had the footwork of a veteran player. The skills that I learned were how I had adapted to the game. I was right wing and my peers trusted me to make a good play. We would walk off of the field sweaty and tired. My sister would spit in her palm and make rude comments to the other players. She also liked to play sports and was bulkier than me. So, we both signed up for baseball as well. A skill that I had learned during soccer was to not allow the ball into my backfield. It was completely by accident that I happened upon this vulnerability of our team. My sister played forward and she was slow. Her weight did not allow her to catch up to the play. I fought like a mad woman to keep the ball from getting past me because I was embarrassed and hurt to see my sister get drilled by the opposing team. Well, in baseball she was bigger and stronger. The boys did not mind having her on the team until she was hit in the arm with a wild pitch. She would never walk onto that baseball field again. I needed her support but stayed on the team although I was terrified of being struck by a ball. My muscle tone was lean. I was also agile and limber. When I was up to bat the crowd yelled, 'Hey batter, batter, batter; swiiiiiiing batter.' The pitch came wildly in my direction without forethought I stretched my lean frame into the shape of a concave circle. The umpire's astonished expression was etched in my memory for life. He called the opposing team's coach over and asked that the pitcher be removed from the game. Sensing commoradery from the team helped to build trust and relationships. Some of the boys would be upset that a girl was on the team and the picked on me mercilessly. My inability to hit a ball brought upon words of encouragement and reassurance from the team. While I was still a part of a softball team my baseball games became a training ground for better improvement to the sport. Eventually, I learned to hit a few good pitches and that was the end of my foray into the sport. Before I left the game my perception of depth had improvement to the point that the glaring sun never interfered with my ability to make a play. My instincts would recall this reflex when my sister was wildly swinging the knife for I only had seconds to react before the blade sank deeply into flesh that was just inches from my heart.

We performed as a trio in the local school talent show and won. We looked like triplets in our matching hats, belts, and clothing. We received a standing ovation and were invited to make a repeat performance before a school wide assembly. Mother made sure that we used the appropriate emphasis and pitch. She wanted us to appear empathetic and draw sympathy from the crowd. My sister was an advice columnists for our school paper. I would write to her to ask for advice about my homework and studies. When we moved to the new private school she was consider to be a troublemaker and began to run away from home. The eldest of the siblings was fare skinned and had dark auburn hair. Her acne was very bad and she was a friendly girl that wore glasses. She resented having so many younger siblings. As she developed into womanhood she became more aloof. When the divorce was taken place she was making future plans that did not include her siblings. Young men began calling our home and stopping by to visit. They would be interrogated about the nature of their visits. They would have to provide proof of license and age. The interrogation did not stop there. They were often asked why they wanted to date her to which they would generally respond that she was pretty. My parents found this to be very shallow and would blatantly tell her that she was foolish for choosing the lad. They reminded her that boys only interested in the outward appearance were also only interested in having sex with her. Oftentimes they would know little more about her than her attractiveness and would not bother to find out anything more unless she would permit them to have sex with her. As devout Christians my parents prohibited any unmarried persons in the family to engage in sexual promiscuity.

When I began to flirt with boys mother was irate. She cautioned me that I would get pregnant and went to extensive lengths to make sure that I would not. In my early childhood years I was never particularly biased to the opposite gender. Papa would say that if a boy messed with me I should pick up the biggest stick that I could find and hit him on the head. When I was raped I remembered Papa's harsh words. It made it easier to cope with the tragedy of being sexually abused. My fear of rejection was crippling my ability to establish relationship. I could trust and believe in Papa because he never misled people into believing falsehoods or lies about the truth.

Being raped leaves a person with physical and emotional scars. A woman blames herself and blocks out the worst feelings of violation and fear that she feels. Part of healing is learning to accept the ugly truth. A man is infinitely stronger than a woman. He over powers her and forces himself upon her. With that he takes with her the most precious part of her life. A father is inclined to protect his daughter at all cost. Fathers are not always there. The presence of a man is domineering and strong. The presence of a woman after she has been raped is feable and weak. There is not an inclination to hide the truth about the rape but, to tell whom? In a day in time of sexual promiscuity would anyone believe me? Is there a law preventing this from happening again? The answer is how to face your new reality. When you are violated by someone learning to trust again is a challenge. Your community is part of the problem that helps the rapist to shield himself behind an effervescent mindset of power. The power to take from someone their life but to leave them with the power to move forward in life. We are a litigious society. Men go to prison and get raped by other men is this justice for their crimes against humanity. Women get raped by men that they may have given a signal. The signal may have been hello. The rapist thinks that women are not to be respected but, to be treated like animals. Black men have been treated like second class citizens all of their life. They are racially profiled by police. They are denied jobs based upon their skin color. Education about rape helps to prevent it from happening to you again. I was not raped by a family member. I allowed a person that I trusted of my same race to abuse me by rape. Responsibility does not fall on the system that rejected the African American demographic to reform the person that raped me. His reformation will be the same as mine. He will have to know that rape is wrong in order to stop him from doing this again.

I have learned to create an equilibrium in my life. To balance love with hate. Hate is too strong an emotion for anybody to feel all of the time. Deep seated resentments are the underlying influence of angry outbursts. I do not have pity for the man either. I do not feel that they should escape justice. Men who rape are the lowest vilest human beings that have walked the earth. I cant help but wonder the commonality that my being raped has with most of the other people of my geography. Will rapists continue to torture innocent victims until they are satisfied? I do not feel safe in my community anymore and I do not look at the world through the rose-colored glasses that I once did. Life for me has new meaning. As a rape victim I am empowered to speak about this to other women. I am empowering other people to speak against it and to prevent harm from happening to themselves and others. By bringing about a change in the mindsets of people that witness crimes everyday, I am becoming a better me one day at a time.

Some women do not respect themselves enough to disallow some of the liberties that men will take with women. These women are either numb to the mistreatment or have grown up around men that have mistreated them. For them it is normal to be referred to as 'bitch' and 'hoe'. It is common for them to refer this way to themselves. The cycle of abuse continues as they have children that are fatherless and they cannot afford to care for them properly. Women are burdened by joblessness and lack of education. Various psychosocial changes are part of the adjustments I had to make in my post rape situation. Secretly, I mourned my soul have been plagued by the tormentor, my rapist. Paradoxically, the African American woman has been the strength and the backbone of their demographic.

I have been mutilated by a knife wielded by my sister. He hatred was beyond her control and she unleashed it one day. I have to forgive people that have hurt me but, I also need to heal. I was operated on and died in the operating room. The doctor's found the bleeding was uncontrollable. I was driving in my vehicle when pedestrians found me slumped over the wheel. They called an ambulance from a nearby payphone and I was rushed to the emergency room. The doctor's performed several tests and found that they would need to operate. The black woman that was assigned to perform the operation did not want to operate and said that if I waited she would run more tests. Mother and my sister were screaming and yelling in the hallway. They bemoaned the doctor's diagnosis and showed their despair at my unfaithful demise. Mother took me home and had the pastor pray over me in a ritualistic way. The prayer lifted my spirits and I was in much need of the operation. The pain never subsided and the bleeding continued to flow freely.

The doctor's prepped me for the operation and in the moments before the surgery Mother explained that I was going die. She cried and clung to me but, I made her smile despite her grief. My reassurance was short lived and panic began to set in. I prayed and prepared for sedation. The doctors told Mother that I lost too much blood and that I died on the operating table. The nurses closed the blinds and my family's faces were sullen. The somber mood pervaded the foggy cloud and my heart wanted to fight to survive another sec. I was in pain and agony. When the medication waned my screams could be heard the length of the hospital floor. Mother stayed by my side day and night pumping in extra doses of morphine to help to numb the pain.

While the doctor saw that I was capable of making a recovery, it was by sheer will. That and the grace of God. He asked me to wiggle my toe. Next, he told me that I was paralyzed and had been in a coma. He instructed me to blink rather than try to speak. I would endure weeks of physical therapy before I could speak and walk again. Mother helped me to rehabilitate from the hospital. After my release she helped me to battle an addiction that I had to the pain medication which was inundated by shakes and hallucinations. Rather than rest and become permanently disabled, I returned to work and school while I was stapled in the abdomen. I prayed that the Lord continue to strengthen me to live. I only weighed ninety pounds and it was painful to walk. My disappointment at having to work was an aspect of my psychological well being. Papa had come to see me while I was recuperating from the surgery in the hospital and his presence was well received. I knew that life was fleeting. It was an indication of how monument us death really is to all of us. He was there to see me live or die and he ministered to me. It was obvious to me the grief that he felt. He struggled to find the words to say good-bye, thought provoking statements that were straddled with grief. The nurses had taken my blood so often that my veins collapsed.

So it was with track marks riddling my arms and stitches and staples in my abdomen that I returned to work at Burger King. Many of my old high school acquaintances were in college and in between summer jobs they found the time to party with local rap stars. My friends that caught the 86 Lithonia to Decatur with me were now signed to LaFace records. Papa negotiated with the local people to get them to perform during a Black History month celebration. My future was still uncertain but, after the party I agreed to return to college and only worked at Burger King part-time. Mother was nearby to help me if I needed anything. She had even bought me a new computer so that I could develop software for my programming classes.

When I returned home pregnant she had the joy of a mother who could share with her grandchild the lasting memories of a dying child. I found out that I wasn't the only family member that had fallen ill. My estranged relative had returned home to live with me and mother. I eagerly help her to rear her new baby. I was also charged with the care of my demented grandfather. He required daily showers, medications, and feeding. He was eighty-six and Mother took him in when he left New York. Gone were all of my uncles and my granddaddy was an old man that needed the support of his family.

My nephew was a delight and a bundle of joy. He was growing rapidly each day when I discovered that I was pregnant as well. My sister had become pregnant with another child. Although, she appeared to be estranged from her husband. Allegations of sexual immorality were speculated about but nothing was to come of it. In my early years, I had been trained that people of my pedigree were immune to gossip. While she hinted that she had contracted something, I simply ignored the inner desire to gossip with her. Even when she blatantly inquired of me as to the location of the local pharmacy, I was disinterested and somewhat curious. Again, she stressed to me with the integrity of a person dying that she must have a pharmacy. I quickly dismissed the urge to ask about the prescription. I was sure that she would probably tell me that it wasn't any of my business. It could have been that she wanted to discuss the topic openly and I shielded her from doing so by distastefully suggesting that the conversation was inappropriate.

Years later, when she was nearly unrecognizable from an infectious disease that caused open blistering sores to seep puss and covered her entire body including her face, she would attempt to have this discussion with me again. I regretted the years that I mistakenly help her to disguise her illness with the hopes that she could lead a semi-normal life. Over the near decade that I lived with her I could have had an opportunity to say good-bye. Instead, the shock from seeing this diseased person, caused me to have heart palpitations so severe that I fell to the floor clutching my chest. She was unrecognizable and I grabbed her shaking her yelling incoherently in her face. I begged the Lord from heaven to spare her the impending doom. Those that were present knew that this was not an   act. But that the close members of the family had orchestrated the surprise meeting. They did not expect this type of reaction and to be fair she had tried to warn me in a sly way.   She had covertly whispered to me at the previous Christmas dinner that it was time. I rejected her last pitiful pleas for help. As a person that had survived HPV I knew that she was had not prepared herself. It was easier for her to hide from the truth and become disillusioned by the prospect of living a long life. Perhaps, she waited for   a cure. Stem cells may have been an ally in AIDS research and it was certain that she had sought the help of German doctor's.

By now I was a bitter aging woman that felt no pity for anyone. I had returned home to live with Papa while he had retired after years of teaching. Man Man was a pro athlete and the lifestyle that went along with that was too much for a young mother to juggle. His sister had returned home after college to stable employment. Finally, for the first time in my life I felt   happy. I had the people in my life that cared about me to support me through a difficult time. Papa was dying as were most of the aunties, cousins, and uncles that had raised me. They would not live long enough to help me to raise my daughter. She brought joy to Papa in his final days. And she brought new life to a man whose wife had divorced him. The same wife also tried to ruin his career. His granddaughter thrived in school. She had the stamina to produce advanced test scores in preparation for a new early college initiative.

This was not the old Mississippi town that I grew up in but was like some new city prepared from the twenty-first century. Youth is fleeting as they say. I prayed that the Lord would forgive me for the sins of my youth. Sessions with a psychiatrist helped me to bring clarity to my thoughts. I once saw chaos and disorder but, now I knew how to take control of my life. By finishing school and working full-time it would help to have some stability. In the process, my daughter would find out about the startling truth of my past. The mistakes of the past can be the cornerstone that you build upon for future success. Cancer hadn't killed me and neither did that knife, but would the underlying legal issues centered around my rape cause me to become a failure?

"For he that sows to the flesh shall of the flesh reap corruption

but, he that sows to the spirit shall have life everlasting"

My college roommate was the sort that had friends from all walks of life. She could not afford things that I had like a new computer and Papa paid my rent so I only needed to work part-time. One day she showed up with a new television set. I asked her how she could afford something so nice. She proceeded to tell me that she had a friend. I was soon to discover who this friend really was. She invited guest over frequently, they would spend the night in the living room or on the floor. I began to ask Papa to change my living arrangements because I felt uncomfortable with the current living situation. She had invited her drug addicted mother to live with us temporarily. Which meant that she would spend nights and leave for days, months, or weeks only to return again. I demanded that she pay hoping that this would motivate her to leave or find work. She did not choose to do either and I argued heatedly with my friend threatening to call the police. Thefts were starting to take place and the police were beginning to step up patrols in our area. Given my race, gender, and community it was only a matter of time before I had to face the inevitable.

Many of the people in our community were of the working class. The Olympics were coming to our state. The classes in technology were revamped to fit the new trends. Many of the professors had chosen to copyright the software that they were developing. In the foreground Bill Gates was earning money hand over fist for his development of Microsoft. I courted a young man from the college and we both began to work for a telecommunications firm. The internship at Oasis

Telecommunications Inc. required me to intern as a operations manager. The work entailed utilizing liasions as well as product brand marketing. I enjoyed the challenging pace and the rewarding incentives.

The office male dominated work force was not without its drawbacks. I began to question the ethics of having an interoffice romance. I still remembered the young man that I had grown up with back at home. The traditional means of courtship were elusive to me as a fresh young executive. It became even more complicated when my first cousin asked me for an entry level position. I hesitantly agreed to permit her to shadow me at the job for a few months just to see if she could get a feel for it. She adapted to the office quite well. After some persuasion from me, she considered changing her major in college. The bond between my family and the gentlemen that I courted was developing quite rapidly. My daughter had taken to the gentlemen and began to refer to him as daddy. Her premature vocabulary was limited to two words, 'daddy' and 'ma-ma".

The woman that babysat for the little girl was a stocky wayward hairdresser. She had retired from working in the local salons and had agreed to keep the child at a minimal rate. City life was expensive. I paid rent, bills, college, and car notes. On a tiny intern's budget that required me to also afford daycare, diapers, and groceries. The babysitter lived a thirty minute drive from my home but on this particular occasion I was stuck in rush hour traffic for nearly an hour. As I pulled up to the drive, she hurled the door open. I was taken aback by the gruff manner in which she had treated me. She informed me that she was upset and would notify the police if I was late picking the child up again. Times like this made me regret not having the luxury of being able to afford reliable daycare. Using my better judgment I advised her that I would no longer be using her services. She pleaded with me to change my mind at which I waved a dismissive hand. As I continued to strap the child in her car seat and turned the woman stood over me holding a heavy object.

I cried out in pain as the marble statue smashed into my nose and forehead. I was not completely unconscious but had suffered a major concussion. Her brother had driven me in my car to the emergency room. The physician questioned me regarding the injury. I couldn't focus on what happened. I felt like I had fallen down a flight of stairs. He informed me that my precious nose had been broken. He persistently asked me to provide him the details of the incident as the police arrested the young man that had taken me to the hospital. I was tired and miserable. The doctor advised that I would need to take two weeks to rest from the concussion and wrote me a referral to a plastic surgeon at the hospital. After that I rested for a week and began to internalize the problems that I was facing.

My job may be given to someone else. This was a competitive job market. I was a value to my team but, the job could be performed by any qualified applicant. My insurance deductible would be expensive and more time off after surgery. I wanted to take some time to travel back home to Mississippi to visit Papa. I really missed him and he was always there for me during times of trouble. I took the pain medication that the doctor had prescribed for me. On a sheet of paper I wrote down the pros and cons of my situation. Living in the city had its benefits and it seemed that my life was moving in a positive direction up until this point.

However, my 'family' were the people that I left back home in Mississippi. I was ready to make a change. I decided to finish school and began searching for jobs close to Papa down near the Gulf. The job offers were not plentiful. I began to give up hope of finding anything worthwhile before my daughter was beginning kindergarten. My face had healed from the scars caused by the violence I had suffered at the hands of the vindictive woman that night. My heart was permanently wounded as I examined the world through the eyes of an infant beginning to develop in a world where people closest to you could cause you undue harm. Children are so innocent and their delicate lives are held in our precious hands. We mold them into curious creatures and they grow into intellectual adults.

She was a delightful child that seemed to be interested in the world around her. She would peer at you from the huge round globes and blink , then blink again. Her mouth moved as it tried to form words. Inaudible sounds would escape the tiny bow mouth. Holding up her fingers she moved the mouth again. This time sound could be heard. One, two tree. She would repeat this again, Oooonneeee ttttwwwwooo, ttttttrrrreeee. As she slowly sounded out each word she would stick up a corresponding finger. I was blown away by her efforts to learn numbers. It was more fascinating when she counted using her fingers. She seemed to understand that numbers were used to count things. However, she was not three she was not quite over the age of one and had recently taken her first steps. There was no denying that this child was developing into a prodigy.

I wonder if the daycare worker had considered the development of my daughter when she took out her anger and frustrations on me. While I had been matriculating at the community college the lecturer began his disertation:

"Domestic violence is prevalent in urban communities. The cause of many to fight in their homes may come from frustration about joblessness. For many, one paycheck may be the difference between a meal and homelessness. The stressors that accompanies the triggers to these stressors causes many to act out violently. The cycle of violence begins to repeat itself as the destruction that it leaves in its wake becomes evident. The victims are mothers, fathers, sisters, brothers, cousins, neighbors, teachers, officers, and preachers. While individuals strive to improve lives by tearing down the strongholds of segregation, others fight to build walls that seal them in purgatory. Lives are permanently marred by incidences of violence. It pervades the thoughts of an oppressed society which is dwindling in poverty. Hoover struggled to oversee a government that was plagued by an era of great depression. People thought that the economy would never cease to exist in perpetuity. There is still hope for America. We must strive in our vocations to provide a rehabilitative effort that is exceedingly and abundantly effectual. The weakness of a democracy lies in its fallacy of perfecting equality. In so much that affirmative action was introduced as legislation that caused for reform in corporations. Society may see this a backwards legislation and deem its efforts as counterproductive. Labeling an individual sometimes may be the predetermined factors contributing to their fate. We as a people find it necessary to place those labels on ourselves. It is our own judgments that preclude misrepresentation of the populus. In schools, there is also legislation that envelopes equality. Public schools are the pre curser to federal legislation that hinges on bridging the gap. Humanity is all inclusive. It is holistic. Improving your daily lives has to be a conscientious effort. Although, this may seem to be undermine by laws and rules that society has placed upon us. There is a moral compass that provides us with a focus on how to begin to make a change. When, where, and how to accommodate the new face of America will take drastic changes. Streamlining the system so that it is not interdependent on departmental guidelines and adjusting our needs so that it meets the needs of the greater good. This will not be done without sacrifice.

Inner city children and rural school children risk their lives to attend public schools. The generation before them did as well. They are doing so for two totally separate purposes. Technology has improved the way that we communicate and this

crosses gender and social barriers. It also appears to be age discriminatory. Leveling the

playing field should be done with a little more ingenuity than meerly, pointing the finger

at your oblivious counterparts and saying the issues lie there. The bible teaches you to

love your neighbor as you do yourselves. This applies when your neighbor is a drug

dealer. When your neighbor is an illegal immigrant that does not pay taxes. This also

applies to the child that is truant. Building back trust in your community will restore the

humanity of the people living within its geographical barriers. People feel rejected by

greedy politicians that seek personal favors through bribery and paid votes. Yet we

become negligent when voting for the democrat or republican that is partial to a certain

value system. Churches are in the political matrix and many wage battles within them by

demanding gay rights and the like. Therefore, the system is adapting to meet the needs of

a society that has a changing value system. Equitable justice systems are unbiased and

more stagnant. The statistics that affect domestic violence are compounding us daily.

According to Merriem Webster's dictionary domestic means : living near or about human

habitations ; of, relating to, or originating within a country and especially one's own

country ; of or relating to the household or the family ; devoted to home duties and

pleasures. This is the epitome of decency. The home is to be valued and this is beyond

the polls and into the living rooms of families. I have learned to become proactive instead

of reactive. I reach out to people that need help and they will sometimes reach out to me.

It is the existential value of any human being to have the right to live, love, and have

peace. Peace is sometimes forsaken by violence."

In the middle of the night sirens blare as they rush to a night club on the strip. The club patrons are milling about the clubs exterior seemingly oblivious to the disruption to the night's affairs. As ambulances arrive the young teenagers scatter to their cars. They have no cares for the casualties and are refusing to provide the police investigators with any helpful information. By the next weekend they will return irregardless of the hazard to their personal health and well being. The club music is a low den as the officers scratch their heads in bewilderment. EMT's arrive and began to perform life saving CPR on one of the nightclub patrons. Blood is pooling beneath the body of a young woman in her early twenties. Shocked employees stand about to witness the gift of life being placed in the hands of the EMT workers performing CPR. The man pumps the chest of the women patiently and firmly attempting to expel a breath from the lifeless corpse. The body is then placed upon a stretcher and covered in a plain white sheet stained with drying blood. Numbness creeps up the spine of the EMT worker as he mirrors the dead stare that is reflected in the eyes of the most recent homicide victim. The silence that embraced him was his own thoughts capturing him in an envelope of peace and serenity. He lowered his head tears poured from the man's eyes. He folded his hands   in prayer. He needed strength from the Lord to help him through this difficult time. The onlookers seeing this gesture of faith took it as an act of kindness and lowered their eyes so as not to meet his gaze. He stared at the expressionless faces of some of the crowd that stood outside the nightclub. He shook his head and his bravery was self evident.

The towns people had asked its city government to stop the violence at the nightclubs. They were going to the polls at the next election to vote on a new curfew that would not allow night clubs to remain open after 1 o'clock a.m. This recent massacre was a dispute amongst rival gang members that were in a turf war for the territory that would soon be turned into a normal place of business. In one final shoot out they had warned the town that nobody was safe from the bloody gang turf war. The bloody battle was sure to ensue once Tyriek found out about Jayshawn snitching on him to the police.

Tyriek had threatened to kill Jayshawn's uncle one night. Tyriek had left home and picked up Jayshawn's uncle promising him a ride. Jayshawn's uncle was never to be seen or heard from again. Jayshawn and Tyriek were rival drug lords that had control of gang territory to the south and east of midtown. They were both competing for control of the new ground that had begun since the recent development of a new co-op. Folks around town had said that Jayshawn's uncle was using more drugs than he was selling and had begun to wander the   streets at night. The club patrons were members of rival gangs. They supported the club by faithfully patronizing the establishment. The murder of Jayshawn's uncle was featured in the local newspaper. That night a famous rap act was scheduled to perform and the club owner's were expecting to triple their usual earnings. Jayshawn should have been at home with his family the night of the concert. He had invested in the club and he promoted the rap group that was scheduled to perform. Tyriek had followed Jayshawn's girlfriend   to the beauty salon earlier. He knew that Lisa only had her hair done by Natalie and only when she wanted to look good. I was in the salon when Tyriek came in there to check on Lisa. He spoke to the ladies and left. Before he left he got a call on his cell phone saying that somebody was looking for Jayshawn's uncle. His reaction is permanently embedded in my memory. He hung up the phone and made another call. The man that he called was a close friend. He and the friend were making plans to hide Jayshawn's uncles body so that it would never be discovered. I was

paralyzed by fear and what I had just heard was a confession to a murder. When I got

home I contacted the witness hotline and reported Tyriek. I felt that it was the right thing

to do and I prayed that the Lord would shield me from any violence. The next morning I

sang with the choir as I normally would do on Sundays. I went home and cooked dinner

for my aunt, uncle, daughter, and Mother. Tyriek's face flashed across the television

screen. He was a wanted man. My heart skipped a beat. I wondered how long it would

take the police to find him. The ladies in the hair salon may not have overheard Tyriek. I

was afraid that he may know that I was the person that informed the police and track me

down. My breath swiftly escaped my lips.   I sat down slowly in my   chair as the

thought raced through my head. This was almost unbelievable. I had to work the next

day. Mother and family left after they finished the meal. We shared some small talk but,

the dinner conversation was less pleasant in lieu of the recent change of events.

The next day at work was not a normal workday I was distracted. My thoughts

were not focused on the present task. I had the feeling that people were watching me.

This was turning into paranoia. I left work at the regular time and drove the usual route.

My daughter leapt from my arms and dashed towards the apartment. I removed the keys

from my briefcase and proceeded to turn the corner in front of the red brick building. As

my eyes adjusted to the dim light, I called for my daughter. She was standing on the

sidewalk staring in the face of the man from the news broadcast. My legs trembled and

buckled beneath me. The fear was tangible in the air. There had been several break ins in

the area. The murder that I had reported was only one of several unsolved deaths that had

occurred within recent years. I could not turn and run. I calmly called my daughter over to me and with as much courage as I could muster attempted to walk past the man in the

walkway. His voice was deep and threatening, " Give me your purse and I won't hurt

you." My eyes searched his face and I pleaded with him to leave me alone. He ordered

me into the apartment and proceeded to force me to the floor. He promised that he would

leave me and the child unharmed if I gave him money. The man smelled of stale whiskey

and cigarettes. His hair was matted in a heap atop his crown. His clothes were filthy

tattered rags. His eyes quickly surveyed the room. They fastened on a large coin jar that

sat on a nearby chest of drawers. "See that is what I'm talking about," said the man.

"Witch you don't need this money." He motioned for me to stay on my knees as he

removed the coin jar. "You need to be more careful," said the man.   He left the door

wide open and dashed down the stairs. I called the police station and asked for the

detective again. He said that Tyriek had been in hiding. I told him about the strange man

and the robbery. "Be careful and lock your doors. Call the front office and notify them of

the robbery. I will have an officer patrol the area. Maybe sometime tonight we will catch

the person who is responsible for all of this," said the detective. He abruptly disconnected

the call. I was in a perpetual state of shock. My daughter appeared to not be as affected

by this as she played with her toys which were strewn haphazardly across the floor.

"Mommy who was that," said the toddler. "Who was who Sweetie," I replied. My

thoughts were dismal. I was somewhat distracted and prepared a list of repairs for the

apartment manager. "That man, mama. He was mean. Mommy, Mommy," she inquired.

"Don't worry, we called the police on the bad man," I said. She was not old enough to

understand but, hopefully the memory would quickly fade. My apartment manager

advised me to move from the apartment as soon as possible. She offered me the lease at another property elsewhere. I declined the opportunity to move to another location. She

gave me the security deposit that I had paid. She wished   me well. We shared a hug. We

were friends and her fiance' was an employee at the company where I had interned prior

to my promotion. She appeared to be worried and I smiled at her reassuringly. I was

concerned for her safety as well. We made promises to keep in touch with each other as I

left her office. My instincts were telling me to be more cautious the next time I met a

casual aquaintence that offered me a place to live.   While leaving her office I mentally

replayed parts of the conversation in my mind. She had mentioned that while I was away

on an extended vacation a family member that I had asked to house sit for me was up to

no good. She said that while she had followed up with him about having a key to the unit,

he was also using my car for his personal enjoyment. To add insult to injury the car

wreck that he was involved in was suspiciously near our home and that he was said to

have been visibly inebriated at the time. She had not reported the accident to police as she

wanted to have an opportunity to notify me first. The worst part about it was the

weeklong house party that he had and completely trashed my apartment. She said that she

had maintenance clean up the mess the Friday before I returned on Sunday evening. I

drove a red sports car and noticed slight damage to the front right fender. There were

very few young African American execs and this car was brand new. The kind of car that

you would most commonly see driven by middle aged women. It was a gift to myself for

the hard work and late night hours. My heart broke when I saw the damage but, it came

with the territory. The precious few young black successful people my age where few and

far between. Most of the peer group were like Tyriek and his crowd. They partied hard

and never came to class. They would steal and buy drugs with every penny that they earned. Employers would not hire them. They would always ask to borrow money from me with the most flimsy excuse. As usual I was suckered into giving it to them. Turning a blind eye to real damage that it caused by me doing so until the world stared me starkly in the face. It was easier to believe that vandals had damaged my car rather than my brother being involved in a hit and run. Since I was out of town it was even more difficult for me to provide an explanation for what had happened. I was still young but, with the added responsibility of motherhood. My friends troubles could cause me to lose this perfect angel that I had given birth to eighteen months before.

Each morning was hectic because I kept a frenetic pace at work as well. She was kicking me in the abdomen but lately I had been feeling hard knots. These were the contractions. I was at Mc Donald's when I used the public restroom and noticed the blood smeared onto the toilet paper. My high school classmate was enjoying my company while pampering me during this pregnancy. She and her cousins were part of another child's birthday party in the restaurant. I whispered to her that I had a feminine problem and her eyes grew big. She breathed, "Is it time,". I replied that is was time and she motioned to her cousin to come over. He offered to take us to the hospital so that it would be faster and less expensive than an ambulance. Mother was prepared with my bag because I knew that I could go at any time. The nurses changed me and got me dressed. The contractions were painful and it was the hardest labor that I had ever had. They coached me through the labor and it was at this moment that the heavens opened up and I welcomed a beautiful baby girl into the world. The doctor's asked me to name the baby. I proudly state Kwanza Dixon. I was exhausted by this time. Doctor's wheeled me to the hospital room. Mother arrived with my belongings and went down to the nursery to visit the baby. Pictures were taken of the infant as she peered at me through the precious eyes of an angel.

Countless well wishers from Mc Donald's donated diapers and clothing for the newborn. They had provided me with a years supply of diapers, formula, and bottles. Since I would not have to shop for the baby for a while, I decided that it was time for me to take some time off from work and prepare myself from motherhood.